C20 0 1709 46 ED

GW01100024

South Eastern Edu

You should return th
which you borrowed it on or before the latest date
stamped be

HEINEMANN

HEINEMANN GUIDED READERS
BEGINNER LEVEL

Series Editor: John Milne

The Heinemann Guided Readers provide a choice of enjoyable reading material for learners of English. The Series is published at five levels – Starter, Beginner, Elementary, Intermediate and Upper. At **Beginner Level**, the control of content and language has the following main features:

Information Control
The stories are written in a fluent and pleasing style with straightforward plots and a restricted number of main characters. The cultural background is made explicit through both words and illustrations. Information which is vital to the story is clearly presented and repeated where necessary.

Structure Control
Special care is taken with sentence length. Most sentences contain only one clause, though compound sentences are used occasionally with the clauses joined by the conjunctions 'and', 'but', and 'or'. The use of these compound sentences gives the text balance and rhythm. The use of Past Simple and Past Continuous Tenses is permitted since these are the basic tenses used in narration and students must become familiar with these as they continue to extend and develop their reading ability.

Vocabulary Control
At **Beginner Level** there is a controlled vocabulary of approximately 600 basic words, so that students with a basic knowledge of English will be able to read with understanding and enjoyment. Help is also given in the form of vivid illustrations which are closely related to the text.

For further information on the full selection of Readers at all five levels in the series, please refer to the Heinemann Guided Readers catalogue.

1

The Examination

One Friday afternoon, I was playing football with my friends. My grandmother called to me. 'Come here, Peter! Come here! Come here quickly!' she shouted.

I ran to her. 'What is it, Grandmother?' I asked.

'Your teacher is here,' my grandmother said.

I was not happy. I felt worried. Why was my teacher here? What did he want? I walked slowly to the house.

My teacher said to me, 'I have good news for you, Peter.'

Then he spoke to my grandmother, 'Peter works very hard at school. He is a very clever boy. I am very pleased with him.'

Grandmother looked at me and smiled. 'Yes, he's a good boy,' she said.

But I was worried. *Why* was my teacher here?

'Peter is very clever,' my teacher said again. 'He can go to Higher Secondary School. But he must pass an examination. The examination is next month. It is a very difficult exam, but Peter can pass.' Then he looked at my grandmother and asked, 'Do you want Peter to go to Higher Secondary School?'

'Go to school in the big town of Trebzin? Go to school in Trebzin?' asked my grandmother.

'Yes,' said the teacher. 'And one day, Peter will become an important person.'

My grandmother looked at me. We had very little money. We were very poor farmers. I had no father and mother. Both my parents were dead and I lived with my grandmother. Grandmother looked after me, but she was very old. She worked very hard.

'But what about money?' I asked. 'What about money for school fees?'

'The examination is also for a scholarship,' my teacher replied. 'Students with a scholarship do not pay fees. There are only ten scholarships a year to Trebzin Higher Secondary School. So only very clever students win a scholarship.'

Then my grandmother smiled. She looked happy.

'Yes,' she said. 'Peter will go to school in the big town. He will go to Trebzin Higher Secondary School. He will not be a poor farmer. He will not live like me. Can you pass the examination, Peter?' she asked me.

'I don't know,' I replied.

'When is the examination?' she asked my teacher.

'The examination is next month,' the teacher said. 'Peter, come and see me tomorrow. I shall explain all about the exam.'

The day of the examination came. There were three papers. The exam lasted all day.

Afterwards, I did not think about the exam. I did not think about the Higher Secondary School. It was the summer holidays and there was no school. I worked hard on the farm and I played with my friends.

Then, one day, the teacher came to my house again. He was holding a letter and he looked very happy.

'Peter,' my teacher said, 'you have passed the examination. And you have won a scholarship. You don't have to pay any fees. Well done, Peter. You are a very clever boy. You can go to the Higher Secondary School!'

My grandmother was very pleased. 'What did I say?' she said. 'You will not be a poor farmer. You are a good boy, Peter.'

'When does Higher Secondary School begin?' my grandmother asked the teacher. 'What must I do now?'

The teacher said, 'You must go to Trebzin Higher Secondary School on 1st August. The official at the school will explain everything. School opens on 2nd August.'

'Yes,' said my grandmother. 'We will go to Trebzin.'

I felt very excited. I was amazed. I was going to Higher Secondary School in Trebzin!

TREBZIN HIGHER SECONDARY SCHOOL

HEADTEACHER: O.H.AMMID

ENTRANCE AND SCHOLARSHIP EXAMINATION

Subject: Mathematics

Complete in BLOCK CAPITALS

Name: PETER SANDA   Age 14

School FEROZ VILLAGE SCHOOL

Place of Birth FEROZ

Date 2nd JULY 19:17

Are you applying for a scholarship YES/~~NO~~

Complete all the questions.

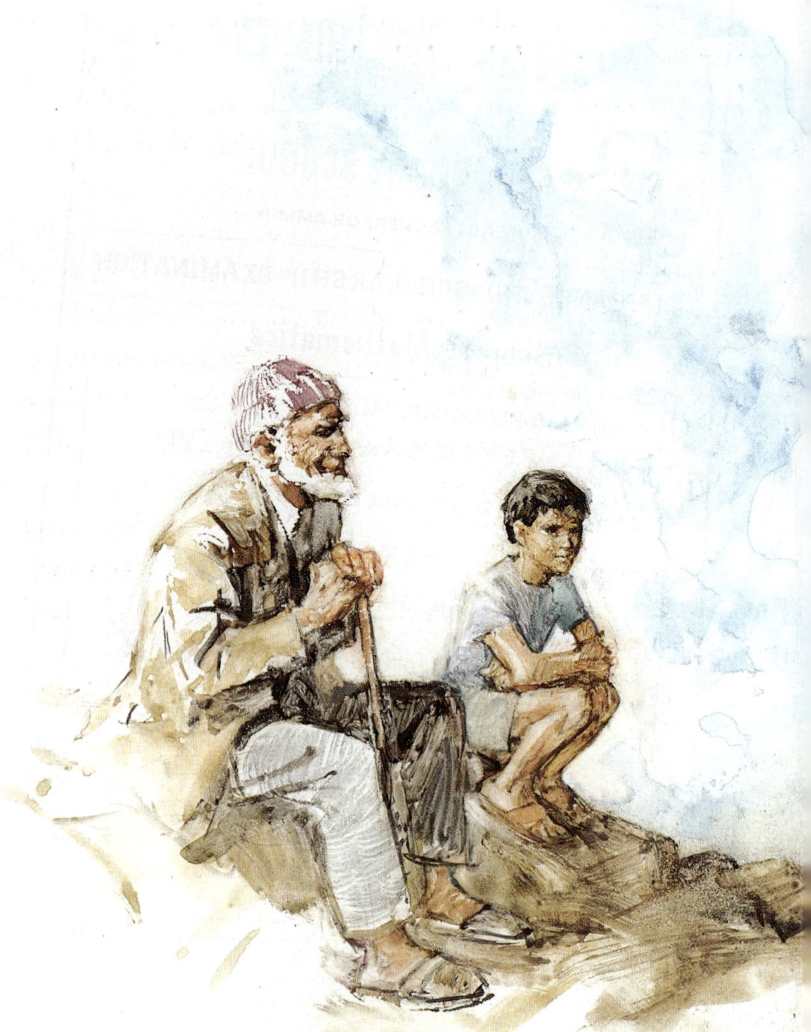

That evening, I visited my old friend, Mr Mark. He was very old and he was like a father or a grandfather. I wanted to tell him my news. I told him about the examination and the scholarship.

Afterwards, we went for a walk and we sat on the hill. We looked down at the village. And Mr Mark told me the story of our village. He had often told me this story.

The people first dug a well and they found water. Then they dug the ground and made fields. They built houses. They always worked very hard. Sometimes the people were happy and sometimes they were unhappy. There were good times and there were bad times. The story of our village was a long story. Lots of things happened to our village.

Finally, Mr Mark looked at me and said, 'Peter, you are now leaving your village. You are going to the town. Never forget your village. Never forget your family and your friends. Never forget the story of your village.'

2

Going to Trebzin

The day came. It was 1st August and we were going to Trebzin. My grandmother and I got up very early. I put on my best clothes and my grandmother put on her best clothes. We were both excited and very happy.

We left our house very early. It was still dark. We walked four miles to the main road. We sat down by the road and we ate our breakfast.

The breakfast was very good. We had eggs, bread and vegetables.

'Thank you, Grandmother,' I said. 'This is my favourite breakfast. It's very good.' My grandmother smiled. The sun was rising.

Then the bus came. After four hours, we arrived in Trebzin.

We walked to the Higher Secondary School. At the gate, we were stopped by the gatekeeper.

'Where are you going? What do you want?' the gatekeeper asked.

My grandmother replied, 'My grandson has a scholarship. School begins tomorrow. We want to see the official.'

The gatekeeper gave a paper to my grandmother. 'Fill in this form,' he said.

> **TREBZIN HIGHER SECONDARY SCHOOL**
> HEADTEACHER: O.H. AMMID
>
> To be completed by visitors at the gate.
> Name: PETER SANDA
> Reason for visit: I have won a scholarship and I want to start school tomorrow.
> Date: 1st August   Signed: Peter Sanda

I filled in the form and gave it to the gatekeeper. 'Wait here,' he said.

After a few minutes, the gatekeeper returned. 'Follow me,' he said.

We followed the gatekeeper to an office. An official was sitting at a desk and reading some papers.

My grandmother said, 'This is my grandson, Peter Sanda. He has a scholarship.'

The official held up his hand and did not look at us. We waited. After a few minutes, the official said, 'What's your name?'

My grandmother replied, 'This is Peter Sanda. He is from Feroz Village School. He passed the examination and won a scholarship. Here is a letter from his teacher.'

The official read the letter. 'Yes,' he said, 'school begins tomorrow at 8 o'clock. His scholarship fees are £150 for each term. There are two terms in each year. His fees for this term are £150.'

13

'£150?' my grandmother asked. 'But he won a scholarship.'

'A *half* scholarship only,' the official replied. 'The scholarship pays half the fees. And you pay half the fees. £150 a term. The *full* fees are £300 for a term.'

'A half scholarship? What's that?' my grandmother shouted. She was angry. 'Does £150 pay for his food and for a room?'

'No, £150 is half of the school fees only,' the official replied. 'Old woman, do not shout at me. Is this boy coming here or not? Tell me now.'

'Yes,' my grandmother said, 'he *is* coming here. He is coming tomorrow. I shall pay the fees every week. I shall work hard and earn the money. And I shall live in Trebzin and look after Peter.'

'Come, Peter,' my grandmother said. 'I don't want to talk to this man.'

We walked out of the office and we walked out of the school. My grandmother was very angry and she was walking very quickly.

'Grandmother,' I said, 'I can't go to Higher Secondary School. We must return to our village. We can't pay the money for the fees. You can't work here. It's wrong.'

My grandmother looked at me and said, 'Peter, you are going to study at the Higher Secondary School. You are not going to be a poor farmer. I can earn enough money. I shall wash clothes. There are lots of rich people in Trebzin. I am old, but I am not finished, Peter. I can still work.'

'Grandmother, it's wrong,' I said.

'Come, Peter,' she replied. 'Where are we going to live? Let's go to Cousin Dev. We will talk to him.'

My cousin, Dev, lived in Trebzin. He worked in a big garage. The garage repaired lorries.

We found Dev at the garage. Grandmother told Dev our story. He was very surprised, but he was pleased.

'Come with me,' Dev said. 'We will talk to Mr Rick.' Mr Rick was the owner of the garage.

We told Mr Rick our story. 'Don't worry,' said Mr Rick. 'I have a shed near the river. It's about a mile from here. You can stay there.'

The shed was very small. But we had somewhere to live.

3

Higher Secondary School

Every morning, I went to school. Every evening, I did my homework. My grandmother worked very hard. She washed and she ironed. Life was hard, but we were happy.

One evening, Dev came to see us. I was doing my homework. 'What are you writing, Peter?' he asked.

'I am writing the story of our village,' I replied. 'Mr Mark has told the story to me many times. I am writing this story down.'

'Read it to me,' Dev said. So I read the story of our village to him. Dev liked it. The next day, I gave my homework to my teacher.

18

A few days later, the teacher gave back my homework. 'Peter Sanda,' the teacher said, 'please stand up. This is a very good story. The writing is beautiful.'

'Thank you very much, sir,' I said.

Then the teacher spoke to all the students. 'Peter's story is about an old man. The old man tells the story of Peter's village. It's very good.' The teacher looked at me again. But now he was angry and he said, 'Peter, you didn't write this story. You copied the story from a book. You cheated.'

I thought of Mr Mark. I thought of our village. I heard Mr Mark's voice and his words. I had not cheated. Mr Mark had told the story, but I had written it. I replied very politely, 'No, sir. I am very sorry. You have made a mistake. I did not copy my story. I did not cheat.'

The teacher shouted, 'Do not argue, Peter Sanda. You cheated.'

I shouted back, 'No! No! You are wrong. I do not cheat. I never cheat!'

I ran out of the classroom. I ran out of the school. I ran into the streets.

I came to Mr Rick's garage. Dev was there. I told Dev about school.

'My teacher says I cheated,' I said to Dev. 'I didn't cheat. I wrote the story. You saw me, Dev. I read the story to you. I didn't cheat, did I?'

'No. No,' Dev said. 'You didn't cheat. Don't worry, Peter. It doesn't matter. You stay here today and you can help in the garage.'

I felt very unhappy. I was afraid to go home and tell my grandmother. So I stayed with Dev.

In the evening, I walked home very slowly. I was very unhappy and very worried.

'What will my grandmother say?' I asked myself. 'What will she think? What can we do? Perhaps I can never go back to school. I will be sent away from school – expelled!'

I came to the river and saw our shed. My teacher was

talking to my grandmother. He was carrying my book. I walked more slowly.

The teacher saw me and shouted, 'Peter! Peter! Come here.'

Then the teacher said, 'I'm sorry. I'm very sorry. I have talked to your grandmother. You didn't cheat. Now I understand. You wrote your story yourself and you are a very clever student.' The teacher looked at my grandmother, 'But your grandmother works very hard. She works too hard. She pays your fees.'

'Yes,' my grandmother said. 'I work very hard. But he's a very clever boy. He will do well.'

'Old grandmother,' said the teacher. 'You work too hard. I shall come back soon and bring good news.'

A few days later, the teacher gave me an envelope. 'This is a letter for your grandmother,' he said. 'Do not open it. Take it home and read it to your grandmother.'

I ran home very quickly. 'Grandmother! Grandmother!' I shouted. 'I have a letter for you.'

'A letter for me?' my grandmother laughed. 'I can't read. Give it to me. I'll open it and you can read it.'

She opened the letter.

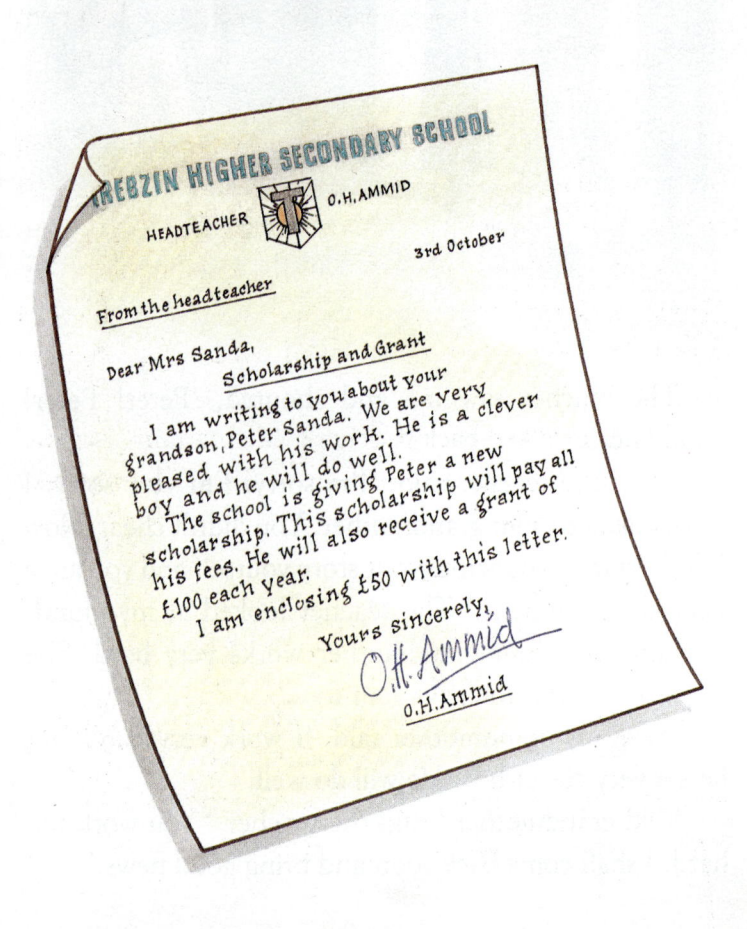

KREBZIN HIGHER SECONDARY SCHOOL

HEADTEACHER   O.H. AMMID

3rd October

From the headteacher

Dear Mrs Sanda,

Scholarship and Grant

I am writing to you about your grandson, Peter Sanda. We are very pleased with his work. He is a clever boy and he will do well.

The school is giving Peter a new scholarship. This scholarship will pay all his fees. He will also receive a grant of £100 each year.

I am enclosing £50 with this letter.

Yours sincerely,

O.H. Ammid

O.H. Ammid

'Fifty pounds?' my grandmother said. 'I don't believe it.'

'Here it is,' I said and I gave the fifty pounds to my grandmother.

Grandmother sat down. She was very surprised and very happy. We laughed and we laughed. We were rich!

'You can stop work, Grandmother. You can retire!' I said. 'No more washing and ironing. Tomorrow, I'll take back the washing. Those rich people can wash their own clothes now. You are going to stop work. You can rest.'

My grandmother smiled. 'This is wonderful,' she said. 'Tomorrow, I shall go back to Feroz village. I shall see everybody. After a week or two, I'll come back. Then we can live in a comfortable house here in Trebzin.'

Next morning, we went to the bus station. We bought a ticket to Feroz. Grandmother got on the bus and I waved goodbye. She looked happy. But she also looked very tired.

Then, I walked back to school. My grandmother was not looking after me. She was not working. She was free. *I* was looking after *her*.

4
Going Home

Each day, I went to school. I worked very hard. In the evening, I did my homework. I was living with Dev, but I thought about my grandmother a lot.

One day, at the end of school, my teacher said, 'There is a letter for you, Peter. A man brought this letter this afternoon.'

I quickly opened the letter and read it.

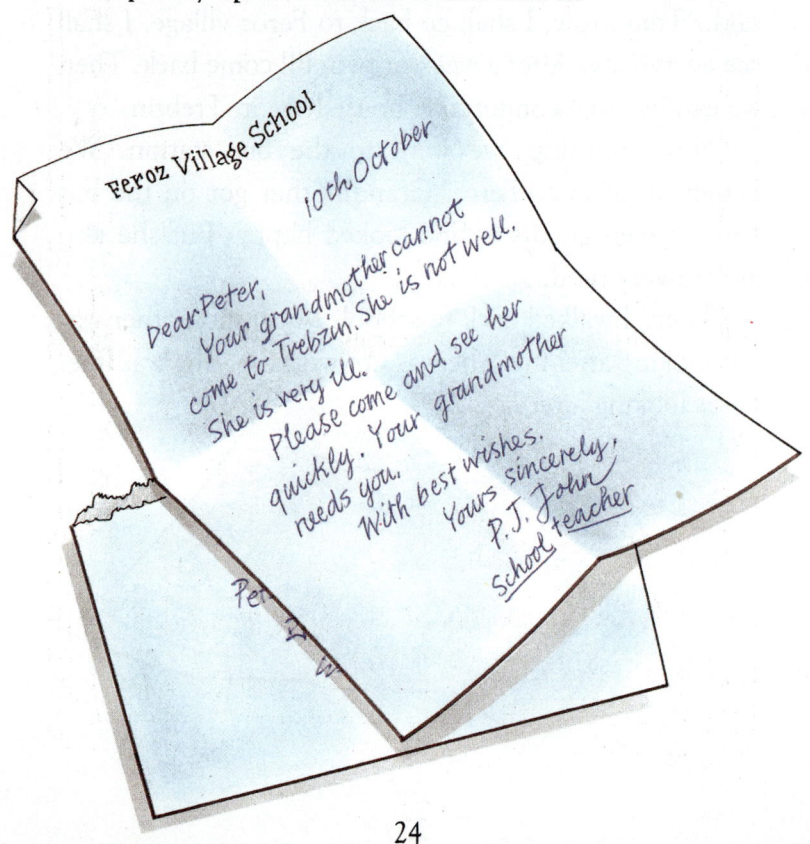

Feroz Village School

10th October

Dear Peter,

Your grandmother cannot come to Trebzin. She is not well. She is very ill.

Please come and see her quickly. Your grandmother needs you.

With best wishes,

Yours sincerely,
P.J. John
School teacher

I ran out of the classroom. I ran out of the school. I ran to the bus station. But it was four o'clock. There were no more buses to my village. I was too late. How was I going to get to Feroz village? What was I going to do?

BUS TIMETABLE

TREBZIN TO MINTA SERVICE

DAILY

TREBZIN TOWN - BUS STATION	7·00	11·00
BLUE RIVER RAILWAY STATION	8·00	12·00
FEROZ VILLAGE STOP	11·00	15·00
MINTA VILLAGE STOP	12·00	16·00
DARPUR TOWN - BUS STATION	15·00	19·00

I ran to Rick's garage. Dev was there and I read the letter to him. 'Dev! What can I do?' I shouted. 'I have to go to Feroz village tonight.'

'Yes,' said Dev. 'You must go. Wait here, Peter. I'll talk to Mr Rick.'

After a few moments, Dev came back. 'Don't worry,' Dev said. 'A lorry is going this evening to a small village near Feroz. You can go on the lorry. And I am coming with you. The lorry leaves at eight o'clock.'

At eight o'clock, Dev and I got onto the lorry. The lorry was full and very uncomfortable. But I was very happy. I was going home to Feroz. I was going to see my grandmother soon.

The lorry was slow and uncomfortable. It was a long journey and we were not able to sleep. At three o'clock in the morning, the lorry driver stopped at a small village. We were ten miles from Feroz. We got down from the lorry and we walked. The moon was shining brightly. Dev and I walked slowly to my village. We were very tired.

After three hours, we came into Feroz. The sun was rising and the birds were singing. We went to my house and my cousin was waiting for me.

'Peter! Peter! You are here! I am so happy to see you,' my cousin said. 'Grandmother wants to see you. She will be so happy. Come in quickly.'

We were so happy. We were home.

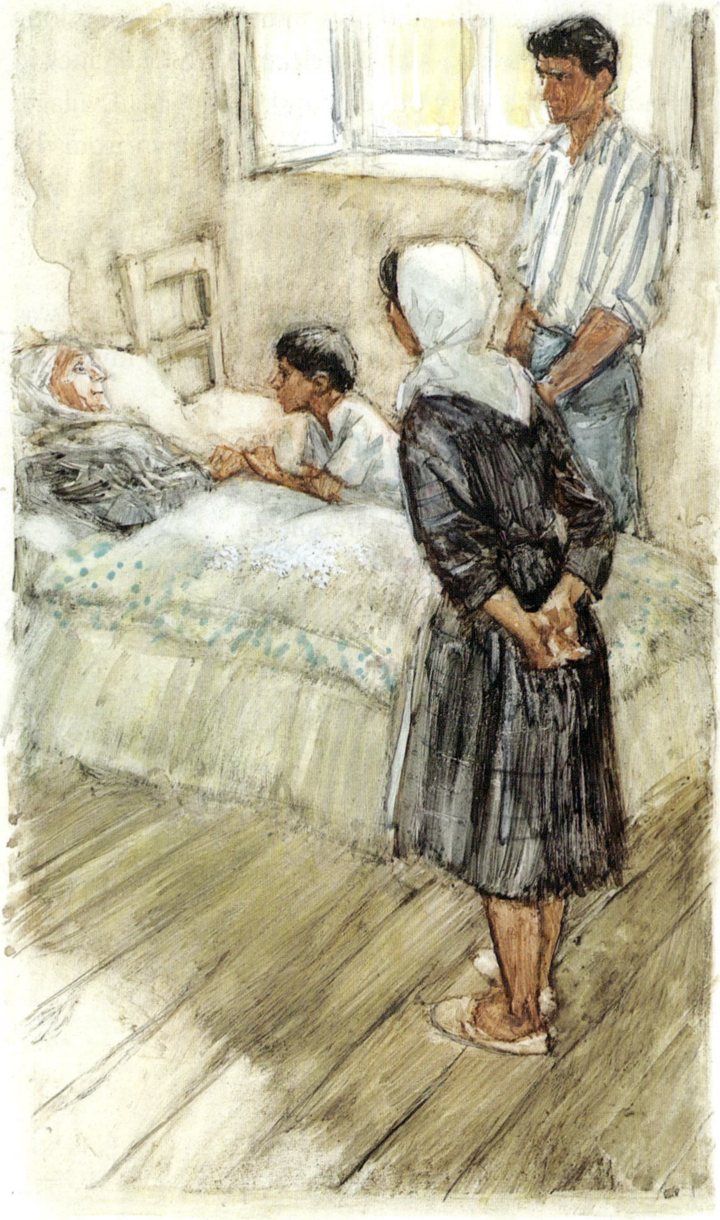

We went into the house. My grandmother was lying on her bed. She was not asleep. She was awake, but she did not look well. She looked ill and very old.

'Grandmother,' I said, 'here I am.'

My grandmother looked at me. 'Peter,' she said, 'you are a good boy. You came quickly.' And she held out her arms to me.

'Grandmother. How are you?' I asked. 'What is wrong?'

'I don't know, Peter,' she replied. 'Yesterday, I was walking in the garden. I was thinking about your Higher Secondary School. I felt happy. Then I felt a terrible pain in my chest.'

Then my grandmother sat up. 'But I feel better now,' she said. 'It's good to see you, Peter. Let's go into the garden.'

Grandmother stood up. I helped her. We walked into the garden. She walked very slowly. We sat down under the tree. Dev and my cousin sat with us. The morning was bright and cool.

Then my grandmother looked at us, and smiled. 'Welcome, Dev. Welcome home, Peter. Peter, do you remember our breakfast on the way to Trebzin? Your favourite breakfast of eggs, bread and vegetables. Let's have your favourite breakfast.'

'Yes, grandmother,' I replied. 'Dev and I are very hungry.'

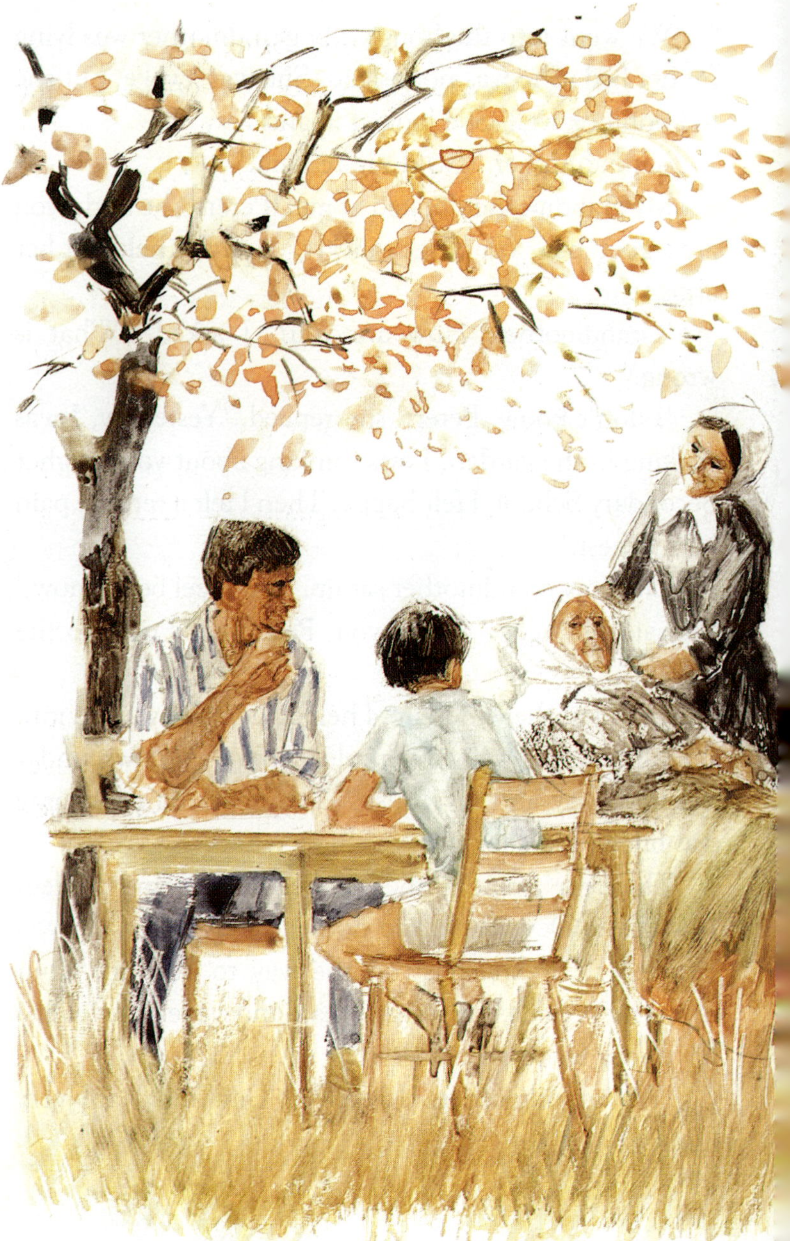

Grandmother smiled again. 'Bring the table,' she said, 'and bring the chairs. You, young people, make the breakfast. I am too tired. I can't work any more.'

We brought the table and the chairs. Grandmother was happy, but she did not look well.

Finally, the breakfast was ready. It was a very good breakfast. Dev and I were very hungry, but grandmother did not eat. After breakfast, she said, 'I am very tired now. I have to go back to my bed.'

We walked slowly to the house again. Grandmother lay down. After a few minutes, I took her hand. Her hand was cold. I looked at her again. She had stopped breathing. She was dead.

―――

That night, Mr Mark was at my house. Many people sat in the garden. Mr Mark told us the story of our village again. He finished the story and said to me, 'Never forget, Peter. Never forget your village and your people.'

'Or my grandmother,' I said.

Heinemann English Language Teaching
A division of Heinemann Publishers (Oxford) Ltd
Halley Court, Jordan Hill, Oxford OX2 8EJ

OXFORD MADRID ATHENS PARIS FLORENCE PRAGUE
SÃO PAULO CHICAGO MELBOURNE AUCKLAND
SINGAPORE TOKYO GABORONE
JOHANNESBURG PORTSMOUTH (NH) IBADAN

ISBN 0 435 27180 6

© T.C. Jupp 1986, 1992
First published 1986
This edition published 1992

All rights reserved; no part of this publication may be reproduced, stored in a retrieval system, or transmitted, in any form or by any means, electronic, mechanical, photocopying, recording or otherwise, without the prior written permission of the Publishers.

Illustrated by Michael Charlton
Typography by Adrian Hodgkins
Cover by Christopher Corr and Threefold Design
Facsimile artwork by Richard Geiger
Typeset in 12/16 pt Goudy
by Joshua Associates Ltd, Oxford
Printed and bound in Malta by Interprint Limited